SILKIE CHICKEN GUIDE FOR BEGINNERS

A SIMPLIFIED GUIDE TO LEARN HOW TO CATER FOR ALL SILKIE CHICKEN NEEDS LIKE CARE, FEED, HEALTH AND TIPS TO RAISE THEM AS LOVELY PETS

RICHARD MARTIN

Copyright © Richard Martin
All Rights Reserved.

This book has been self-published with all reasonable efforts taken to make the material error-free by the author. No part of this book shall be used, reproduced in any manner whatsoever without written permission from the author, except in the case of brief quotations embodied in critical articles and reviews.

The Author of this book is solely responsible and liable for its content including but not limited to the views, representations, descriptions, statements, information, opinions and references ["Content"]. The Content of this book shall not constitute or be construed or deemed to reflect the opinion or expression of the Publisher or Editor. Neither the Publisher nor Editor endorse or approve the Content of this book or guarantee the reliability, accuracy or completeness of the Content published herein and do not make any representations or warranties of any kind, express or implied, including but not limited to the implied warranties of merchantability, fitness for a particular purpose. The Publisher and Editor shall not be liable whatsoever for any errors, omissions, whether such errors or omissions result from negligence, accident, or any other cause or claims for loss or damages of any kind, including without limitation, indirect or consequential loss or damage arising out of use, inability to use, or about the reliability, accuracy or sufficiency of the information contained in this book.

Made with ❤ on the Notion Press Platform
www.notionpress.com

Contents

Title Page

SILKIE CHICKEN GUIDE FOR BEGINNERS

A simplified guide to learn how to cater for all silkie chicken needs like care, feed, health and tips to raise them as lovely pets

Richard Martin

CHAPTER ONE

Introduction to Silkie Chickens

Silkies are one of our favorite breeds, what's not to like? They have a beautiful and abundant feathering, like cuddling, and are really loving. Whether you're on the silkie bandwagon or not, we guarantee that by the conclusion of this post you'll have some stunning new silkie additions to your backyard flock faster than you can say brilliantly beautiful bantams!

Lifespan

The lifespan of a normal silkie chicken is from 7 to 9 years, however this depends on the care they get. Some Silkies are known to live longer than average, so give them a little extra TLC and you'll enjoy their devotion for many years!

Class of silkies

The silkie is a real bantam with feathered legs, meaning they are only available in bantam (miniature) size and have abundant feathering covering their legs - a magnificent sight!

Rarity

They are a common breed, so acquiring one of these magnificent birds should not be difficult.

Origin of silkies

Originating in Southeast Asia, most likely China.

History of Silkies

These magnificent birds originated in China before to the year 1200 and were appropriately called due to the silky texture of their feathers. Marco Polo, who traveled across Asia in the 13th century, described Silkies as "chickens with fur-like feathers" in his trip journals. In 1874, the North American Standard of Perfection included Silkies into its ranks. We are fortunate to currently locate silkies all over the world and in several backyard flocks!

Fun Facts about silkie chickens

- Unlike other chickens, who have white skin, silkies are noted for their black or dark blue skin. This is a peculiar trait, to be sure, but it's just one more thing that makes this breed so special.
- Silkies have a natural maternal instinct and have been seen sitting on the eggs of various species, including ducks and turkeys - a true mother hen!
- Chickens have an outstanding UV cone in their eyes that allows them to see many more hues and colors than human eyes do; this is extremely useful while searching for insects and other delectable treats on the grass. This UV cone enables the silkie to detect the health of her

chicks. Developing feathers reflect UV light, allowing the silkie to know which of her chicks are growing well and which ones need further care.

Enter Caption

Current Use or Function

Silkie hens are mostly raised in suburban backyard flocks for the aim of becoming a fascinating and pleasant companion animal. In addition to being a popular display bird, their remarkable beauty also makes them an attractive addition to your flock. Silkies are particularly popular because they are excellent mothers and will frequently sit on the eggs of less maternal birds until they hatch - ideal if you want to produce a large number of chicks for many years.

CHAPTER TWO

What is silkie Chicken

Silkies have, contrary to popular belief, existed for ages. There are records from academics and explorers who may have painted these magnificent birds as early as the thirteenth century, if not earlier.

Some claim that Aristotle described them in some of his works when he spoke to "birds with fur like cats," but the most often cited source is Marco Polo's writings and descriptions from his trips in China. In fact, it is believed that here is where the bird evolved.

While the bird's silky feathers and slate-black skin, flesh, and bones have stayed constant, other characteristics, such as available colors, comb form, and crest size, have developed and altered throughout the years, particularly as the bird's popularity has increased.

According to the 14th Edition (2020) of the American Bantam Association (ABA), Silkies are the fourth most popular bantam breed in the United States.

What does a Silkie chicken look like?

In general, a well-bred Silkie should have a comb in the form of a walnut, a medium-sized, soft, and full crest that is more globular on the female and more erect on the male, with feathers extending from the rear.

The eyes should be huge, brilliant, and very dark in hue, while the beak should be short, wide, and well-bent.

The lobes of the ears are turquoise, and the neck is short and proportionate.

The bird's back should be short and wide, and its tail feathers should be plentiful, soft, and well-curved, with adequate shredding at the ends.

Medium-sized wings should be held tight and almost horizontally. The mane, face, and wattles should have a dark mulberry hue.

Depending on the hue of the feathers, the shanks and toes should be black to slate blue, and the bird should have five toes.

These characteristics, in addition to a list of finer nuances and the lack of DQs or faults, would constitute your ideal bird - the one that every professional breeder strives to develop.

ABA only acknowledges birds with silky type feathering in black, blue, buff, gray, paint, partridge, self blue, splash, and white in bearded and non-bearded variants, with the exception of paint, which is only recognized as a bearded variety.

What Is a Silkie Showgirl?

Showgirls and Strippers, often known as Naked Neck Silkies, are available in a variety of colors and all three feather styles.

The only distinction between a Stripper and a Silkie is the lack of feathers down the length of the neck.

A Showgirl's neck is devoid of feathers, but she has a bowtie-like bib of feathers that covers the lower neck and upper crop region. White-bearded Showgirls are the only Naked Neck Silkie presently recognized by the ABA.

Enter Caption

Black showgirl

Why Do humans raise Silkie chickens?

The majority of owners of Silkie chickens maintain them as pets. Their calm and pleasant disposition makes them an ideal companion for families with children. Silkies are very docile and simple to domesticate. Many may even get used to sitting on your lap.

With adequate care and health management, Silkies may live between 7 and 9 years.

Silkies do lay excellent white to tan eggs of medium size, but they are not renowned for their production, therefore most do not depend on them exclusively.

This is mostly a result of their persistent broodiness. And I mean it when I say I am persistent. They just like sitting on eggs! Some may even nest without an egg underneath them! This makes them excellent incubators, and many people utilize them to birth other bird species.

Enter Caption

Young Wet Silkies

Are Silkies Difficult to care for?

Silkies may provide some unique obstacles, but with a few modifications to the normal chicken care regimen, they are rather simple to maintain.

CHAPTER THREE

What is silkie Chicken

Silkies have, contrary to popular belief, existed for ages. There are records from academics and explorers who may have painted these magnificent birds as early as the thirteenth century, if not earlier.

Some claim that Aristotle described them in some of his works when he spoke to "birds with fur like cats," but the most often cited source is Marco Polo's writings and descriptions from his trips in China. In fact, it is believed that here is where the bird evolved.

While the bird's silky feathers and slate-black skin, flesh, and bones have stayed constant, other characteristics, such as available colors, comb form, and crest size, have developed and altered throughout the years, particularly as the bird's popularity has increased.

According to the 14th Edition (2020) of the American Bantam Association (ABA), Silkies are the fourth most popular bantam breed in the United States.

What does a Silkie chicken look like?

In general, a well-bred Silkie should have a comb in the form of a walnut, a medium-sized, soft, and full crest that is more globular on the female and more erect on the male, with feathers extending from the rear.

The eyes should be huge, brilliant, and very dark in hue, while the beak should be short, wide, and well-bent.

The lobes of the ears are turquoise, and the neck is short and proportionate.

The bird's back should be short and wide, and its tail feathers should be plentiful, soft, and well-curved, with adequate shredding at the ends.

Medium-sized wings should be held tight and almost horizontally. The mane, face, and wattles should have a dark mulberry hue.

Depending on the hue of the feathers, the shanks and toes should be black to slate blue, and the bird should have five toes.

These characteristics, in addition to a list of finer nuances and the lack of DQs or faults, would constitute your ideal bird - the one that every professional breeder strives to develop.

ABA only acknowledges birds with silky type feathering in black, blue, buff, gray, paint, partridge, self blue, splash, and white in bearded and non-bearded variants, with the exception of paint, which is only recognized as a bearded variety.

What Is a Silkie Showgirl?

Showgirls and Strippers, often known as Naked Neck Silkies, are available in a variety of colors and all three feather styles.

The only distinction between a Stripper and a Silkie is the lack of feathers down the length of the neck.

A Showgirl's neck is devoid of feathers, but she has a bowtie-like bib of feathers that covers the lower neck and upper crop region. White-bearded Showgirls are the only Naked Neck Silkie presently recognized by the ABA.

Enter Caption

Black showgirl

Why Do humans raise Silkie chickens?

The majority of owners of Silkie chickens maintain them as pets. Their calm and pleasant disposition makes them an ideal companion for families with children. Silkies are very docile and simple to domesticate. Many may even get used to sitting on your lap.

With adequate care and health management, Silkies may live between 7 and 9 years.

Silkies do lay excellent white to tan eggs of medium size, but they are not renowned for their production, therefore most do not depend on them exclusively.

This is mostly a result of their persistent broodiness. And I mean it when I say I am persistent. They just like sitting on eggs! Some may even nest without an egg underneath them! This makes them excellent incubators, and many people utilize them to birth other bird species.

Enter Caption

Young Wet Silkies

Are Silkies Difficult to care for?

Silkies may provide some unique obstacles, but with a few modifications to the normal chicken care regimen, they are rather simple to maintain.

CHAPTER FOUR

Incubating & Hatching

As silkies are renowned for being highly broody and excellent moms, many opt for natural incubation rather than conventional methods. Silkies will patiently wait on her eggs until they hatch, displaying a strong mother instinct and assisting her offspring in every way she can. However, since silkies have a thick "under fluff," it is possible for newborn chicks to get entangled in these feathers, resulting in their death.

If you are incubating your own eggs, verify that your incubator has an exact humidity control, since this has been shown to effect the hatchability of silkies. Aside from this, incubation should be same to that of other breeds. Silkies may demand more care and effort throughout the hatching process. They often have a thicker shell membrane, which, in conjunction with their bigger head and feet, might make the hatching process more difficult and delicate. If they seem to be struggling to make progress after pipping, you may need to assist the chick as much as possible without speeding or pressuring the process more than necessary. However, this is not a regular occurrence, and the majority of silkies will hatch like pros!

Egg Behaviour

While silkies aren't renowned for their ability to produce eggs, they are fairly excellent and consistent layers, producing around three exquisite small cream eggs each week. Even if their eggs are little, don't let that deter you; they are just as tasty and healthy as ever! If you're fortunate, you'll even have fresh eggs on your breakfast table throughout the winter, since their feathers will frequently keep them warm, satisfied, and producing eggs throughout the season.

Silkie Roosters

In fact, it is more difficult to establish the gender of a Silkie than it is for many other breeds, and this is particularly true when the chicken is young.

A fundamental distinction between a silkie hen and a silkie rooster is size. Roosters are bigger than hens, and their wattles and combs are larger and more rounded. Silkie roosters have unusual feathers in addition to their fuzzy feathers. These longer, more pointed, and more robust feathers resemble those of other birds.

You may also observe crowing as an indication that your chicken is a rooster, however this is not always the case.

How silkies Appear

The silkie is renowned for its highly distinctive and imposing look. Its silk-like plumage is so soft and fluffy that it has been mistaken for rabbits. Silkies possess a lot of characteristics that are uncommon in other chicken breeds, including five toes (instead of four) and dark blue or black skin, bones, and earlobes - such a fascinating breed!

Silkies may be either bearded or unbearded, have a walnut-shaped comb, and are also crested; the feathers encircling their heads are often so abundant that you cannot see their amusing tiny faces. Their magnificent feathering even covers their legs, so it's no surprise that they are often compared to a huge pompom!

Black, blue, buff, white, partridge, splash, and gray are recognized variants.

Additional Variations include scarlet, lavender, porcelain, and cuckoo.

Enter Caption

CHAPTER FIVE

Caring for silkies

Silkies, like all other hens, need a certain amount of care to keep them happy and healthy. While they are not a high-maintenance breed, because to their delicate and significant feathering, they do require a little additional care to keep them looking very intelligent and sassy.

Bedding

Bedding is required for silkie chicks. There are several accessible bedding materials, so add bedding to the coop. Wood shavings are an excellent bedding material for silkie chicks.

In addition to straw, sawdust, hay, sand, newspaper shredding, and pine needles, you may also explore other materials. Remember that not all mattress materials are same, and some are superior than others.

Enter Caption

For instance, wood shavings are very absorbent but hay is not. Sand is simple to clean but is seldom used (because chicken owners generally face many problems with using sand as their bedding).

Feeder and Waterer

Add enough feeders and water containers to accommodate the quantity of chickens.

Purchase a water feeder instead of filling a container with water, since there is a possibility that the chicks would drown if they fall in.

Nesting Boxes

Maintain a few nesting boxes inside the coop for your silkies. If you grow silkies as pets, it is recommended to keep one box per bird.

Provide an Environment Free of Predators

To successfully raise silkie hens, you must protect them from predators. Because silkies can't defend themselves and the feathers on their heads might impair their vision, you must guarantee that their coop is predator-proof or that they are housed in a predator-proof coop.

The silkies also need shelter from severe weather conditions (such as snow, hail, wind and rain). During the summer, they also want shade and a cool spot to shelter themselves from the heat.

Consider installing a heat light inside the coop to keep the birds warm throughout the winter months.

Grooming

Silkies will dust bathe and preen themselves to maintain their pristine appearance, so they do not need further care. If your fluffy companions do get dirty, a simple rinse and pat dry will do the job! However, it is essential to examine them periodically for lice, mites, and other parasites; with more feathers comes additional responsibility!

CHAPTER SIX

How to Feed Silkie Chickens

Silkies need no particular diet; to keep them in fighting shape, give them a balanced, protein-rich diet of seeds, grains, and vegetables. When they are approaching the stage of laying, they should be given a specialized "layer feed" to ensure they get all the nutrients they need to produce an abundance of tasty eggs.

Watering

Ensure your silkies have access to an adequate quantity of fresh, clean water. Daily refilling of the water containers is required. Additionally, the container should be cleaned at least once every week.

Tips and Caution

• Contact a veterinarian or take your birds to one if you see indications of disease (such as loss of appetite, depression, sneezing or abnormal stool).

• Keep a watch out for hostile behavior in your flock and separate the hens that cannot get along. When chickens in a flock have dominance conflicts, they may often hurt one another.

• To prevent a fire from starting in the coop, remove any bedding, cobwebs, and debris from near the heat lamp or any electrical equipment.

Depending on the temperature, you might consider employing heat lights throughout the winter. This will help your birds stay warm. Additionally, heat lights will prevent the water in the coop from freezing.

• Ensure that your coop has enough ventilation. Ensure a sufficient water supply during the summer to avoid dehydration.

In the event of a mite infestation, replace all bedding. Also, dust the new bedding with diatomaceous earth to eliminate fleas, mites, and lice.

• As a result of their smaller size, silkie chickens may benefit from smaller grit.

• Ensure the safety of your birds from all forms of predators.

CHAPTER SEVEN

Housing your silkies

Silkies, like all other hens, need a sturdy coop to protect them from the weather and annoying predators. It should be made of durable wood, with a galvanized wire mesh, and secure locks to keep out unwelcome guests. As they like to sit on their eggs often, the coop should have many nesting boxes that are attractive, roomy, and draft-free. Roosts are also an essential component of a silkie's house, although they should not be too high off the ground since silkies have difficulty flying. Silkies are energetic little birds who need space to stretch out their fabulously feathered legs, so ensure that their habitation includes a run or fenced-in area for them to explore.

Health Problems

Silkies are not known to have any health concerns beyond those of a typical chicken. However, owing of their fluffy feathers, they are sensitive to mite and lice infestation, thus it is essential that they are periodically inspected for parasites. If parasites are present, ensure that they are correctly treated, either by yourself or by a veterinarian, since these infestations are known to spread and may result in major health problems for your hens. Dust bathing is essential for preventing lice, mites, and fleas, therefore make sure your flock has access to dust bathing facilities. Since with other hens, make careful to regularly deworm your silkies, as this is another condition that may be fatal if left untreated.

Hardiness

Silkies may have the disposition of lovely, submissive little darlings, but don't be deceived; they are still regarded as a very robust and resilient breed! They are able to thrive in both cold and warm climates due to the insulation provided by their attractive plumage. Be mindful, though, that silkies feathers are more like fur and not waterproof like other chicken breeds, so if you live in a tropical area, you will need to provide them with adequate cover and protection. Due to their tiny size and inability to fly, they tolerate confinement well. However, if provided with enough room, they make excellent use of it and are excellent foragers, able to find delectable morsels from long distances!

Enter Caption

Why Do We Adore Them?

I feel it is abundantly clear that we like silkies and believe they are an essential element to any backyard flock! However, if we must put it in paper, here are the top five reasons why we are so enamored with amazing silkies and why you must get them immediately.

1. While we're usually the kind to judge a book by its cover, it's difficult to resist the silkie's fluffy plumage! The silkie's appearance is more elegant than that of a typical cat or dog.

2. Do not overlook all of its insane unique chicken characteristics, like its black-blue skin and appendages, five toes, feathered legs and beards; it is not your average red hen!

3. They adore you in return! Silkies like human connection and will follow your every move in the yard, doting on you. Whoever said chickens couldn't be affectionate was obviously wrong!

4. They give you with an abundance of wonderful tiny eggs on a steady basis. They may not be as huge as your ISA Brown's eggs, but they are as tasty (and healthy) - eggs-cellent for tiny mouths!

5. With a personality as sweet as honey, silkies are difficult not to fall in love with! You might be excused for assuming that they are high-maintenance birds, considering their looks, yet these adorable birds are everything but. Being so docile and placid makes them a joy to care for, and their kind and kind attitude makes them an outstanding pet!

CHAPTER EIGHT

Where Can I Buy a quality Silkie Chicken?

If you are looking for a really beloved and lovely Silkie for your backyard, a Silkie breeder will be your best bet. Too frequently, I encounter dissatisfied owners who have raised chicks with tender loving care, only to end up with a chicken that vaguely resembles the adorable poofs they saw when they fell in love with the breed. Purchasing from a local feed store or a large operation mail-order hatchery may result in an unsatisfactory bird.

Find a breeder in your area and discuss your objectives with them. Question them about their birds. Do they appear? If not, are their birds bred according to the Standard of Perfection? (SOP.)

A breeder that adheres to the SOP will nearly always have accessible pet-quality birds from their hatchlings. These are chicks or young adults that the breeder does not want in his or her breeding facilities because to certain flaws or characteristics. It might be an incorrect number of toes, a lack of or the wrong color markings, the absence of a beard, light-colored eyes, or an asymmetrical wing. A breeder will "cull" for a variety of factors, the majority of which will be entirely undetectable to a beginner. They will be affordably priced, well-kept, and of a superb quality overall.

If you want to become a serious breeder in the future, mention this with your breeder so that he or she may assist you in selecting beginning birds that match your future objectives. While it will likely be difficult to get a bird of actual show caliber, they may have adults or juveniles who were near but did not make the cut for whatever reason.

What is the price of a Silkie chicken?

Realize that the breeder has put many hours and a substantial amount of money into bringing these birds to this stage, and the price will reflect this. The pricing range for chicks will be between $10 and $30 while the price range for adult birds will be between $40 and $100 or more. These numbers may be lower or greater depending on the breeder's competence and time/financial commitments, as well as the bird's geographical location, color, quality, and age.

While we're discussing acquiring excellent birds (and the soaring popularity of Silkies in general), I'd like to bring up a "buyer beware" situation for your consideration. Please investigate the breeder before acquiring hatching eggs, chicks, or adult birds from anybody claiming to sell "show grade" birds. If they are claiming to have "show quality," they should be currently displaying or have shown in the recent past.

Buying eggs or birds from someone who acquired show-quality breeder birds from someone else is not necessarily a purchase of show-quality products. A breeding operation requires many hours of record keeping, dozens of hatches, and several alterations to produce a single animal fit for the showroom.

In light of this, at the absolute least, how can someone claim to have show-quality birds if the birds they produce have never been evaluated by a judge? So please be mindful of what you are purchasing.

The world of Silkie chickens is a constantly evolving hobby. Whether you are looking for a few pets for your backyard or pondering the possibility of becoming a show fancier in the future, there are numerous options to consider. Enjoy the trip and have a great time along the way!

The End

If you are looking for a really beloved and lovely Silkie for your backyard, a Silkie breeder will be your best bet. Too frequently, I encounter dissatisfied owners who have raised chicks with tender loving care, only to end up with a chicken that vaguely resembles the adorable poofs they saw when they fell in love with the breed. Purchasing from a local feed store or a large operation mail-order hatchery may result in an unsatisfactory bird.

Find a breeder in your area and discuss your objectives with them. Question them about their birds. Do they appear? If not, are their birds bred according to the Standard of Perfection? (SOP.)

A breeder that adheres to the SOP will nearly always have accessible pet-quality birds from their hatchlings. These are chicks or young adults that the breeder does not want in his or her breeding facilities because to certain flaws or characteristics. It might be an incorrect number of toes, a lack of or the wrong color markings, the absence of a beard, light-colored eyes, or an asymmetrical wing. A breeder will "cull" for a variety of factors, the majority of which will be entirely undetectable to a beginner. They will be affordably priced, well-kept, and of a superb quality overall.

If you want to become a serious breeder in the future, mention this with your breeder so that he or she may assist you in selecting beginning birds that match your future objectives. While it will likely be difficult to get a bird of actual show caliber, they may have adults or juveniles who were near but did not make the cut for whatever reason.

What is the price of a Silkie chicken?

Realize that the breeder has put many hours and a substantial amount of money into bringing these birds to this stage, and the price will reflect this. The pricing range for chicks will be between $10 and $30 while the price range for adult birds will be between $40 and $100 or more. These numbers may be lower or greater depending on the breeder's competence and time/financial commitments, as well as the bird's geographical location, color, quality, and age.

While we're discussing acquiring excellent birds (and the soaring popularity of Silkies in general), I'd like to bring up a "buyer beware" situation for your consideration. Please investigate the breeder before acquiring hatching eggs, chicks, or adult birds from anybody claiming to sell "show grade" birds. If they are claiming to have "show quality," they should be currently displaying or have shown in the recent past.

Buying eggs or birds from someone who acquired show-quality breeder birds from someone else is not necessarily a purchase of show-quality products. A breeding operation requires many hours of record keeping, dozens of hatches, and several alterations to produce a single animal fit for the showroom.

In light of this, at the absolute least, how can someone claim to have show-quality birds if the birds they produce have never been evaluated by a judge? So please be mindful of what you are purchasing.

The world of Silkie chickens is a constantly evolving hobby. Whether you are looking for a few pets for your backyard or pondering the possibility of becoming a show fancier in the future, there are numerous options to consider. Enjoy the trip and have a great time along the way!

9 798889 863816

Printed by Libri Plureos GmbH in Hamburg,
Germany